Title

Middle/High School

by
Walter A. Hazen

Published by Instructional Fair
an imprint of
Frank Schaffer Publications®

Instructional Fair

Author: Walter A. Hazen
Editors: Sharon Kirkwood, Kathryn Wheeler, Lisa Hancock

Frank Schaffer Publications®

Instructional Fair is an imprint of Frank Schaffer Publications.

Send all inquiries to:
Frank Schaffer Publications
3195 Wilson Drive NW
Grand Rapids, Michigan 49534

The Industrial Revolution—middle/high school

ISBN: 1-56822-780-9

4 5 6 7 8 9 10 MAZ 10 09 08 07 06

Table of Contents

Introduction

The Industrial Revolution that began in the 1750s in Great Britain was more correctly an industrial "evolution." It was the striking acceleration of developments and changes that had begun to take place several hundred years before.

During the Middle Ages, most goods were produced in craft guilds. But as the Middle Ages drew to a close and modern times began, guilds declined in importance and production shifted to the home. This was especially evident in the making of cloth. A system called the *domestic system* took hold, and "cottage industries" throughout England spun thread and made cloth to satisfy the ever-increasing demand for cotton products. The domestic system continued until it could no longer meet demands. Soon machines became so large and powerful that factories had to be built to accommodate them.

The Industrial Revolution brought about many changes. Factories replaced home workshops as the way goods were produced. Trade, transportation, and communications were stimulated. Cities grew and their populations exploded, resulting in social problems that continue even to this day. Child labor became common, and children as young as four years old worked 12-hour days in textile mills. Some were even chained to their machines to prevent them from running away.

The Industrial Revolution that began in Great Britain spread to America at the end of the eighteenth century. It constituted the first phase of industrialization in the United States. A second phase began after the Civil War. The advent of the first transcontinental railroad spurred the growth of other industries, resulting in "robber barons" such as Cornelius Vanderbilt, Andrew Carnegie, and John D. Rockefeller leaving their marks on the American economy. This second phase also produced revolutionary changes in transportation, communication, and other areas. It was also accompanied by social evils, not the least of which was a continuation of child labor. But it nevertheless led to an increase in the standard of living for many Americans.

In truth, the Industrial Revolution is an ongoing occurrence. New inventions and ways of doing things are constantly changing the ways goods are produced and distributed. Modern technology has certainly rendered invalid the suggestion by a number of Americans in the early 1900s that the U.S. Patent Office be closed because everything that could be invented had been, and the reason for the office's existence was no longer valid!

As with other books in the *Eye on History* series, most units of *The Industrial Revolution* begin with a letter, diary or journal entry, or newspaper account that either describes or is related to an event that actually took place. Although the entries are fictitious, they address subjects that people of the times were reflecting upon and discussing. Each unit or segment of the book concludes with topics for debate, research, or discussion designed to challenge students' critical thinking skills.

The Eye on History series strives to bring history to life through the personal experiences of those who lived them. The more students are able to experience history through what others may have felt and thought, the more meaningful it will be. After all, history is not just musty dates and facts. History is the stories of individuals and nations and of heroes and ordinary people We hope this series will help students understand history in new and exciting ways.

Liverpool, England
September 5, 1771

Dear Diary,

Each day I sit at this spinning wheel, often working long after sunset to meet Mr. Newton's demands. The new loom makes it difficult for us to keep up. The weavers keep calling for more thread, but we are hard pressed to supply it.

Things were different just a few years ago. I had time to pursue other endeavors, and working at the wheel by the fireplace was a pleasant task. Now it has turned into an impossible burden, and I have little time for myself. Even though Father is understanding and sympathetic, he still must have the thread ready when Mr. Newton comes calling.

Am I destined to spend my life at this demanding wheel? Will I ever have time for love and romance? I sometimes worry that I shall never marry and have a family of my own.

The fictitious diary entry above might well have been written by a young lady living in eighteenth-century England. Many girls spent their entire lives at the spinning wheel, and as a result, never married. Because a girl who spun thread at a spinning wheel was known as a "spinster," in time the term came to describe an unmarried woman, or "old maid."

The Industrial Revolution did not occur overnight. Factories did not just spring up, and workers did not suddenly appear to fill them. The process took place over a long period of time. But what gave impetus to industrial development in the eighteenth century was a tremendous increase in the population of Europe between 1750 and 1800. Such huge increases stimulated trade and led to a greater demand for goods.

Although small shops had long existed to produce such goods as silverware, jewelry, and hardware, the Industrial Revolution began in the textile industry. A decrease in imported cotton products from India spurred the growth of the industry in England. Why England? England possessed both the damp climate and the mineral resources needed for the production of cotton cloth. She also had the capital and an overseas empire from which to draw raw materials.

One of the first inventions to harbinger the coming of the factory system was John Kay's flying shuttle in 1733. It enabled a weaver to weave cloth at twice the speed as before, putting pressure on home spinners to meet the increased demand for thread. This latter need was met with a patent in 1770 by James Hargreaves, who invented a new spinning machine he called the *spinning jenny*. Hargreaves named his machine after either his daughter or his wife, depending on which source one chooses to believe. Regardless, the jenny could produce eight times as much thread or yarn as the traditional spinning wheel.

Both the spinning jenny and the flying shuttle were small and hand-operated and, like the spinning wheel and hand loom, could be used in workers' homes. While these so-called cottage industries met demands at first, it wasn't long before larger and more powerful machines appeared on the scene.

Discuss . . .

- what it might have been like for a young person to work all day and evening at home at one task.
- possible reasons (other than an increased birth rate) for the rapid growth of population in Europe after 1750.
- what new social class appeared as a result of the Industrial Revolution.
- why some undeveloped nations today have yet to experience an Industrial Revolution.

Leicester, England
June 3, 1785

My dearest Sister,

Circumstances are forcing us to move to Nottingham and take employment in the mill there. Much as we wished not to, we finally accepted the fact that we cannot remain at home with our wheel and loom. These abominable factories are driving us all to the poorhouse. The Chatsworths and the Bradfords are also relocating to Nottingham. Families can no longer compete with the mills and their infernal machines.

I don't worry for Niles and me, or even for Thomas. Thomas is a strong boy and should have no problem adjusting to working in the mills. But I worry for Elizabeth. She is only six years old, and frail. How will the long hours and the stifling atmosphere of the factory affect her? In spite of our fears, we have no choice but to take her into the mill with us. Besides, the pay is so low that it will take the work of our whole family just to put bread on the table.

I often envy you and your life on the farm. I know times are hard for you and John also, but at least you have food and can enjoy the fresh air. Maybe someday we can put aside enough money to purchase a small piece of land some place. At least we can still dream.

Give my fondest regards to John and to my nieces and nephews.

Your loving sister,
Abby

In what was called the domestic system, entrepreneurs supplied spinners and weavers with the materials to turn out products in their homes. The entrepreneurs then paid the workers for the finished products and took it upon themselves to find markets in which to sell them. The domestic system worked well until two developments rendered it outdated. First, the demand for cotton cloth became so great that home industries could not satisfy it; and second, newer and larger spinning and weaving machines were built that were driven by water power, necessitating the building of factories near rivers and streams to house the machines.

In 1769, Richard Arkwright, an English inventor and manufacturer, patented a new spinning machine called the *water frame*. However, when Arkwright invented his water frame, the machine had to be installed in a mill with an available source of water power. So shortly afterward, he built the first English cotton mill that combined several manufacturing innovations in one operation. Other mills soon followed, and the factory system began.

Arkwright's invention was soon followed by another spinning machine called the *spinning mule*. Invented by Samuel Crompton, the mule combined the features of the spinning jenny and the water frame, thereby replacing those two machines. Suddenly the tables were turned, and there was so much thread available that the weavers could not keep up.

A healthy balance between spinning and weaving was once more achieved in 1786, when Edmund Cartwright invented the steam-powered loom. A factory worker operating the water-driven power loom could more easily keep up with the supply of thread.

A separate unit is devoted to the revolutionary invention in the United States of the cotton gin by Eli Whitney, which speeded up the production of cotton products even more.

Discuss . . .

- the impact of machines on skilled labor.
- why eighteenth-century society saw nothing wrong with small children working in factories.
- which machine mentioned above was of greatest importance in the development of the factory system.
- why workers sometimes sabotaged machines.

Mulberry Grove
Savannah, Georgia
February 3, 1793

My dear Father,

An unexpected turn of events has brought me to Mulberry Grove, the plantation home of Mrs. Nathanael Greene just outside Savannah. Mrs. Greene is the widow of that General Greene who fought with such distinction in the War for Independence. Mulberry Grove was a gift to the general from the grateful people of Georgia.

I met Mrs. Greene on a schooner while I was en route to accept a tutoring position with a family in South Carolina. But, upon hearing that the pay was not what I expected, and having secured no alternate position, I accepted an invitation from Mrs. Greene to be her guest for a short stay at Mulberry Grove.

The invitation from my hostess has opened up new possibilities for my future. One night, at a large dinner party Mrs. Greene gave for a group of local planters, the conversation turned to cotton and the difficulties of turning it into a profitable crop. The problem, everyone acknowledged, was not a lack of demand for the product. There is demand aplenty, especially from the cotton mills of England. But a difficulty lies with removing the seeds from the cotton fibers. The type of cotton grown in Georgia and South Carolina is of the short-staple variety, which I understand requires many hours of hand labor to clean. The gentlemen present told me that one slave working all day can process only one pound of cotton. An entire family working by the fireside at night, and assisted by their household slaves, could only manage several pounds by bedtime.

As the table conversation continued, Mrs. Greene, knowing me to be a tinkerer of sorts, encouraged me to avail myself of her workshop. She seemed to feel I might be able to invent a machine to remove the seeds from the cotton fibers. I set to work immediately, and in ten days had contrived a rough working model, consisting of a wooden cylinder with wire teeth that successfully combed out the seeds. Mr. Phineas Miller, Mrs. Greene's plantation manager, has agreed to back me financially. It seems the next step is to return to the Northeast with a view to obtaining a patent.

I must close, as Mrs. Greene expects my presence at another dinner party tonight. Please convey my love and regards to Mother.

Your son,
Eli

Continued on page 8.

With Eli Whitney's cotton gin, our story of the Industrial Revolution shifts for the moment to the United States.

The advent of the cotton gin (gin for "engine") had a tremendous impact on both America and the entire world. Until its invention, some Southern planters had contemplated giving up on cotton as a cash crop. The difficulties in processing it for sale far outweighed the financial gain derived. Some growers even talked of setting their slaves free.

Everything changed when the cotton gin was put to use. A slave using the machine could clean up to 50 pounds of cotton a day, compared with the 1 pound previously accomplished by hand. And with a larger gin that was later driven by water power, one slave could remove the seeds from 1,000 pounds of cotton in a single day. Almost overnight, the production of large acres of cotton became a profitable reality. In less than two years, the amount of cotton exported by the South rose from 140,000 pounds to 1,600,000. More than 4,500,000 bales were being produced by the time of the Civil War. This huge output accounted for two-thirds of the world's total production. And most of it found its way to the flourishing cotton mills of England.

By 1790, England was importing 30 million pounds of cotton a year to keep the machines in its cotton mills humming. Twenty years later, largely because of Eli Whitney's cotton gin, that number had increased fourfold. It is not difficult to see the impact that Whitney's invention had on the Industrial Revolution.

What was a boon for Southern planters and British factory owners proved to be a sentence of slavery for thousands of innocent Africans. With cotton becoming a major cash crop because of the cotton gin, more and more slaves were needed to pick it. Just a few short years after Whitney produced his machine, an additional 20,000 slaves were imported to work in the cotton fields of Georgia and South Carolina alone. When this number was added to the thousands of others put to work on cotton plantations in neighboring states, the South had in excess of 3.5 million slaves by the time the Civil War broke out in 1861.

Discuss . . .

- whether Eli Whitney realized the impact his invention would have on the institution of slavery.
- what effect the cotton gin would have on mill workers in England.
- whether the cotton gin would result in higher or lower prices for cotton goods produced in British factories.

For Debate

Resolved: Had it not been for the cotton gin, slavery in the South would have died out in time.

Journal Entry
February 4, 1744

    I am concerned about that nephew of mine. Even though he is sickly and confined to his room much of the time, it appears he dawdles far too much. I have advised his parents that the lad should be reading good books or pursuing other intellectual endeavors.

    How does young James Watt now bide his time? In such useless pursuits as watching a boiling kettle! I have observed him staring at the kettle for what seems like hours, completely transfixed by the force of the steam lifting the lid up and down. Occasionally he will hold a spoon at the spout and marvel as the steam condenses into water. The lad is utterly consumed! I begin to wonder if he is feeble-minded.

James Watt was not the first person to be fascinated by steam and its potential power. Hero of Alexandria, an ancient scientist, actually built a small steam turbine between the first and third centuries. But since the Egyptians and Greeks had an abundance of slaves to do their work for them, they simply laughed at the thought of any kind of labor-saving device.

Interest in steam power continued through the Middle Ages and into the modern era. The first practical use of steam power came about in 1712 when an Englishman named Thomas Newcomen built a steam engine to pump water from coal mines. Although the engine worked, it was far from cost-effective. Its huge appetite for fuel used almost as much coal as it helped to mine.

Young James Watt was working as an instrument maker at the University of Glasgow in 1763, when one of Newcomen's machines was brought to him for repair. Watt studied the engine and hit upon a way to improve it. To Newcomen's machine, which worked by forcing steam into a hollow cylinder to move a piston back and forth, Watt added a condenser with an air pump. He also added a steam jacket to maintain the necessary heat in the cylinder. The result was that Watt's engine shot steam into both ends of the cylinder, causing it to move at a much faster rate. Whereas Newcomen's slow-moving engine was practical only as a pump, Watt's new device offered all sorts of possbilities for the future.

Watt was granted a patent for his steam engine in 1769. Five years later, in 1774, he received the backing of Matthew Boulton, a Birmingham manufacturer. This sent Watt on his way to financial success, and by the time he retired in 1880, he was a wealthy man.

By 1785, Watt's steam engine had replaced water power in some of England's cotton mills. The engine also made it possible to build factories in places other than next to rivers and streams. Thus, factories could be located in cities where a large supply of cheap labor was available for work. By 1804, an engine similar to Watt's was being used to run Richard Trevithick's steam locomotive. And, three years later, Robert Fulton's steamboat, the *Clermont,* driven by steam engine, chugged up the Hudson River from New York City to Albany at the breath-taking speed of almost 5 miles per hour!

Something to Think About

Many historians consider the steam engine the most important invention of the Industrial Revolution. Write a paragraph telling why you agree or disagree with this contention.

Discuss . . .

- how ill health may drive persons such as James Watt to succeed.
- others in history who have achieved fame in spite of physical challenges.
- what means of power would eventually replace the steam engine.

At Sea

June 13, 1790

I imagine old Jedediah Strutt would tear me from limb to limb if he knew my whereabouts. Little does he know that I departed Belper for London with the plans for his machines tucked away in my head. When I reached London, I told everyone I was a farm laborer on my way to America to seek my fortune. No one suspected that I was, in truth, an overseer from the cotton mill at Belper on the run.

Samuel Slater left England in 1790, having successfully executed a bit of industrial espionage. His crime? He had memorized plans for constructing the spinning machinery necessary to open a textile mill in the United States.

Between 1750 and 1800, England had a monopoly on the production of cotton cloth by machines. The Industrial Revolution had begun in England, and the English were determined that it should stay there. Parliament passed laws designed to keep spinning machines and the plans for making them within the boundaries of their island nation. There was even a law that forbade anyone who had worked in a cotton mill from leaving the country.

Samuel Slater was apprenticed to a cotton mill at the age of 14. Through dedication and hard work he advanced to the position of overseer. Thinking America the ideal place for launching his own enterprise and possessed with a phenomenal memory, he studied and memorized, for use in America, the mechanics of the spinning machines in his place of employment. Then, at the age of 22, he set out for the United States to build a factory of his own.

Slater's cotton mill was not the first spinning factory to be established in America. Several years earlier, factories using easily copied jennies had appeared in Philadelphia and other places. But Slater's mill was the first that proved to be a success.

With financial backing from financier Moses Brown, Slater launched his cotton mill in a former clothier's shop at Pawtucket, Rhode Island, in December 1790. The factory drew its power from the waterfalls of the Blackstone River. At first, the going was a little difficult. The water around the water wheel often froze, and Samuel himself would crawl upon the ice and break the sheets to permit the wheel to turn. His experience that first winter left him with rheumatism, an ailment that plagued him for the rest of his life. But the young industrialist persevered and soon added other mills to his business holdings.

Slater's mill was a factory that only spun thread. It did not weave that thread into cloth. All weaving in America was still done in homes on hand looms. Twenty years passed until the first cloth-weaving mills appeared. These mills evolved in almost the same way as Slater's mill at Pawtucket.

In 1810, Francis Lowell, a gentleman with a memory equal to Slater's, took a two-year tour of England. While there, he visited factories and studied the machinery used to both spin and weave thread. Consigning what he saw to memory, he returned to the United States and opened his own

Continued on page 11.

mill at Waltham, Massachusetts, in 1814. The mill was the first anywhere that spun thread and wove cloth under one roof. After his death in 1817, Lowell's business partners changed a small village named East Chelmsford into a mill town and re-named it Lowell after their former associate.

Thanks to Samuel Slater and Francis Lowell, the Industrial Revolution in America was underway. It started in New England for the same reasons its European forerunner had started across the Atlantic. New England had the right climate and an abundant supply of water power to make cotton mills feasible. It also had a large supply of labor. After years of trying to wring a living out of New England's rocky soil, thousands of farm workers moved to factory towns. By 1840, some 50,000 people were employed in cotton mills and woolen mills throughout the region.

From the textile mills of New England, the Industrial Revolution spread to other areas and industries. Some of these will be addressed in the next unit.

James Hargreaves' "Spinning Jenny"

Discuss . . .

- what might have happened to Samuel Slater if his plans to come to America had been discovered.
- whether you would have had the courage—as did Samuel Slater—to leave a secure job in England for an uncertain future in America. Why or why not?
- why early factories were built near waterfalls.
- whether you would have helped finance Samuel Slater's first mill. Why or why not?

Coalbrookdale, England
March 14, 1736

Dear Father,

Today I witnessed firsthand how coke is made at the Coalbrookdale works. It is a relatively simple process that can easily be duplicated at your foundry in Birmingham.

There is actually only one step in the making of coke. Coal is stacked in heaps and partially burned in the open air. I am told that all the natural gases are driven off by the heat. What is left is almost pure carbon. This, when burned, produces the intense heat necessary to successfully smelt iron ore. And it burns without creating a lot of smoke.

Abraham Darby seems unconcerned that his method of producing coke might leak out to others. Perhaps this is because the coal Darby uses contains very little sulphur. The less sulphur, the less chance of the resulting iron being brittle.

I will tell you more of what I have learned when I arrive home in a fortnight. Until then, give my love and regards to Mother and Julia.

Your son,
Reginald

Once the Industrial Revolution was in full swing, it gave impetus to other inventions and developments. The process was like a chain reaction. The need for machinery in factories led to an increased demand for iron to make those machines. And to meet the demand for more iron, a better and cheaper way had to be found to mine and smelt it. To do this, more coal was needed to produce the coke that made the fire that smelted the ore. At the same time, additional coal was need to operate the steam engines that drove the machines in the factories and pushed the locomotives along the tracks.

In the early 1700s, the smelting of iron ore was accomplished with charcoal. Charcoal was obtained by burning wood. As with the making of coke from coal, hardwood logs were stacked in a heap and burned. But this time the heap was covered with dirt. Just enough air was admitted to keep the wood burning without it bursting into flames. After about five days, the wood would be *charred* instead of totally consumed by the fire. Hence, the term *charcoal*.

Charcoal was an excellent fuel for smelting iron ore. The problem with using it was that there was always a limited supply of wood. Wood was used for many purposes in the eighteenth century, not the least of which was to build the many ships that served the English nation. This limited availability of wood is what led Abraham Darby to try the use of coke at the Coalbrookdale Works in England in 1735. Many ironmakers, however, found coke-smelted iron too brittle to work. It wasn't until Darby's son, Abraham II, refined the process in 1750 that coke smelting took off.

Discuss . . .

- why pure coal is not used for smelting iron ore.
- how iron differs from steel. Which is better?

For Further Study

How is iron converted into steel?

Something to Think About

The Greek philosopher Plato asserted that "necessity is the mother of invention." Do you think this was true regarding many of the inventions that appeared during the years of the Industrial Revolution? Explain.

The Steamboat: Fulton's Folly

Tavern Gossip
New York City
August 21, 1807

I confess that I was one of those skeptics who stood on the banks of the Hudson several days ago and hooted as "Fulton's Folly" prepared for its maiden run.

Why, the fool thing looked like a sawmill on fire—smoke belching skyward like a furnace gone mad! I half expected the contraption to blow up and send all those posh ladies and gents aboard off to meet their Maker.

My doubts were almost confirmed at the start. The boat's engine roared to life, the paddle wheel turned, and the monstrosity began to move. Then it stopped. All was quiet except for the crowd on shore, which commenced to shout and laugh and point with glee.

Mr. Fulton himself, I hear tell, went below and tinkered with the engine. Probably kicked the tarnation out of the thing! But whatever he did, it came to life anew, and the boat lurched forward. I just heard that it reached Albany in the span of 32 hours!

The chain reaction of inventions that characterized the Industrial Revolution also brought about changes in transportation. One of the first to appear was the steamboat.

The steamboat, like many inventions, was not the work of one individual. Inventors had been trying to come up with a practical steam-driven boat for years. Many developed plans and some even sought patents. Two Americans, John Fitch and James Rumsey, even came close to blows one day in the streets of Philadelphia over rights to the steamboat. Fitch was the first to launch such a boat in 1787, a full 20 years before Robert Fulton. His boat was equipped with long, canoe-like paddles on each side, but it was powered by a steam engine. Unfortunately for Fitch, the public was not ready for the era of the steamboat, and he was unable to turn his venture into a profitable business.

Enter Robert Fulton. A painter turned inventor, Fulton was actually more interested in submarines than steamboats. He worked on such a boat for about 10 years and succeeded in building one that could stay submerged for six hours at a depth of 25 feet. Fulton even managed to blow up several anchored test craft while demonstrating his invention. But to his dismay, no government would commit to funding his submarine plans.

In 1802, Fulton received the financial backing of Robert R. Livingston, the United States minister to France, to build a steamboat more practical than the one previously built by Fitch. Fulton succeeded in 1807, naming the craft the *Clermont* after Livingston's home on the Hudson River. It proved to be a commercial success, launching the great age of steamboats that lasted in America until after the Civil War.

Discuss . . .

- possible reasons why Fulton succeeded where Fitch and others had failed.
- what means of navigating rivers were utilized before the advent of the steamboat.
- why earlier river craft were disassembled and sold for lumber at the conclusion of a trip downstream.
- why people often believe that new ideas or inventions will not succeed.
- whether you would take a trip on any previously-untested means of transport. Why or why not?

Schenectady, New York
August 10, 1831
Dear Jonathan,

What an exhilarating day! The De Witt Clinton negotiated the 16 miles between Albany and Schenectady in exactly 46 minutes. Can you believe such speed? Why, I understand the train averaged almost 3 miles per hour! Who would have thought such was possible—especially considering it was pulling five coaches packed to capacity?

From my room at the inn, I reflected on the events of the trip. Fear and apprehension of the unknown were tempered somewhat by a number of humorous, albeit frightening, occurrences. These began just as soon as the train departed from Albany.

First, the locomotive lurched forward with such a jerk that hats were separated from heads and bodies were tossed to the floors of the coaches. There followed some complaints, but most passengers took it all in stride. Then, after everyone had settled back for the ride, soot from the engine soon began to blacken the skin and clothing of everyone on board. But this was nothing compared with what happened next. Burning sparks from the engine's stack entered the coaches, and everyone engaged in a game of dodge—all to no avail. A few ladies opened umbrellas to ward off the sparks, but these soon caught fire and had to be thrown out the windows. One or two unfortunate souls shrieked upon finding their clothing afire, and much commotion ensued while others on board worked feverishly to douse the flames. No one suffered serious injury, and all aboard were laughing and chatting away by the time the locomotive reached its destination.

Hundreds of cheering spectators lined the track when the De Witt Clinton screeched to a halt, its historic journey complete. Cannon were fired and speeches made. I tell you, Brother, it was quite an event.

Travel upon a locomotive as soon as you have the opportunity. I can promise you it will be an experience you will not quickly forget.

Your brother,
Richard

By the time the *De Witt Clinton* made its maiden run from Albany to Schenectady, a number of locomotives were operating on both sides of the Atlantic. There were short lines running between points in the southern and eastern United States, as well as between several cities in England. All this occurred a quarter of a century after the first steam locomotive appeared in England in 1804.

Continued on page 15.

Credit for the steam locomotive's invention is usually given to Richard Trevithick. Trevithick, an English engineer, built a locomotive in 1804 that pulled five wagons containing ten tons of iron and 70 passengers. It traveled a distance of nine miles at a speed of 2 1/2 miles per hour. Trevithick later built another locomotive he dubbed *Catch Me Who Can*, which he exhibited in London on a circular track. Resembling more a merry-go-round than a train, *Catch Me Who Can* enjoyed a brief success because of its novelty. Trevithick tried his railroading luck in Peru, but after some success a revolution there shattered his plans, and he returned to England a broken man.

It was left to George Stephenson to make the locomotive a commercial success in England. In 1814, he built a steam locomotive he called the *Blucher,* which pulled a train of eight passenger cars at a speed of 4 miles an hour. Fifteen years later, he turned out an improved locomotive called *The Rocket*. Unlike the *Blucher* and other early locomotives which barely crept along, *The Rocket* could attain a speed of 29 miles per hour. That was viewed as extremely fast in those initial days of railroading. For his contributions, Stephenson is often referred to as the "Founder of the Locomotive."

The first steam locomotive to run on rails in the United States was built in 1825 by John Stevens. Stevens, an inventor and engineer, built the locomotive at his own expense and demonstrated it on a circular track at his home in Hoboken, New Jersey. Four years later, the *Baltimore and Ohio* began operation as the first railroad line in America. It was on this line that inventor Peter Cooper unveiled his tiny engine, the *Tom Thumb*.

You are probably familiar with the story of *Tom Thumb*. The engine was so named because it was little larger than a handcar. But it could reach a speed of 15 miles per hour, convincing many that railway travel was practical. The fact that it once lost a race with a horse did not dampen the public's enthusiasm for it. After all, *Tom Thumb* was in the lead until its engine temporarily failed.

By the end of the 1830s, rail lines were operating not only in England and the United States, but in other European countries as well. The age of railroads had begun.

Make a Time Line

On a separate sheet of paper, create a time line showing the milestones in railroad history listed below. Consult an encyclopedia or book on railroads for specific dates for some events.

Place the following on your time line: Stephenson's *The Rocket*; Trevithick's locomotive; Peter Cooper's *Tom Thumb*; Watt's steam engine; first sleeping car; transcontinental railroad in U.S.; mail first carried by railroad.

Washington, D.C.
May 24, 1844
What hath God wrought?

Simple though it was, the above was the first message ever relayed by telegraph. It was sent by Samuel F. B. Morse over a line that extended 40 miles from the U.S. Supreme Court room in the Capitol in Washington to Baltimore, Maryland. Two days later, news that James K. Polk had accepted the Democratic Party's nomination for president at their national convention in Baltimore reached Washington over the same line. The age of telegraphic communication had begun.

The groundwork for Morse's telegraph had been laid almost a half-century earlier, in Europe. Count Alessandro Volta, an Italian physicist, built the forerunner to the electric battery in 1800. In the 1820s, André Ampère, a French scientist, explained the laws governing the magnetic effect of an electric current. Using the knowledge gained by Volta and Ampère, Morse built and tested his first telegraph in 1837, after running ten miles of wire around his room in New York City.

Six years after Morse sent his first message from Washington to Baltimore, an underwater cable was laid from Dover, England, to Calais, France, successfully connecting England with continental Europe. Then in 1866, the famous Atlantic Telegraph Cable linking America with Europe was laid. Other cables followed, making it possible for Queen Victoria of England, on the occasion of her sixtieth year on the throne, to send a message to her subjects in forty distant parts of the British Empire:

"From my heart I thank my beloved people," the queen wired by touching an electric button in her palace. "May God bless them." Within minutes replies had come from Canada, Africa, and Australia.

Even before Morse's telegraph became a reality, other advances in communication had occurred. In 1814, steam power was applied to the cylinder press, speeding up the process of printing. In 1828, Noah Webster came out with the first comprehensive American dictionary. And in 1839, Louis Daguerre, a French inventor and painter, perfected what came to be called the daguerreotype process of making photographs. Daguerreotype pictures were printed on thin copper plates. Their greatest disadvantage was that they had no negative. If several pictures of the same setting were requested, the same pose had to be duplicated a number of times. Pictures you see that were taken before 1850 were all daguerreotypes.

For Further Study

The names of scientists and inventors such as Volta, Ampère, Watt, and Ohm are associated with electrical terms today. Do you understand what the words *volt*, *ampere*, *watt*, and *ohm* mean? Write a brief definition of each.

Discuss . . .

- why Morse might have chosen "What hath God wrought?" as the first message to be sent over a telegraph line.

- which method of communication you consider the greatest ever devised.

- what advances in communication will most likely occur in the future.

- what means of communication were employed before the Industrial Revolution.

Lawrence, Kansas

October 14, 1834

Today I read with interest the article in "Mechanics' Magazine and Register of Inventions and Improvements" about the reaper machine recently patented by Mr. Cyrus McCormick. I must say I am impressed with the machine. I can't help thinking about the changes it could make here on the farm.

Mr. J., an associate of mine, saw McCormick first demonstrate his reaper three years ago. Even in its earliest stages, the machine could harvest from 10—12 acres of wheat a day. I compare that with my best day working a scythe with a cradle: 3 acres.

This reaper machine, along with the new steel plow, seems to be pointing the way to a new way of farming and harvesting.

Coinciding with progress in transportation and communication were new advances in agriculture. Among these were the steel plow, the reaper, the mechanical binder, and the steam-driven thresher. The first two—the steel plow and the reaper—had the most profound effect on agriculture in America in that they helped open the Great Plains to extensive farming.

Pioneers who began pushing into California and Oregon in the 1840s bypassed the Great Plains as uninhabitable. Rain was sparse, and the soil seemed unsuitable for farming. The "Great American Desert," as they called it, was best left to the Indians.

Then John Deere invented his steel plow in 1837. Previously, farmers had gotten along quite well with plows made of wood and iron. But wooden and iron plows could not handle the matted roots characteristic of the prairie grass of the Plains, nor the sticky soil surrounding these roots that clung to the blades and made plowing difficult. Deere's steel plow easily cut through the difficult prairie grass and its gluelike soil. Suddenly, cultivation of the Plains seemed a possibility.

But even with the steel plow, farming vast areas of the Plains was not practical because of a shortage of manpower. Using cradles and sickles, many workers were needed to harvest grain and similar crops, and there just were not that many settlers living in the region. McCormick's reaper solved that problem. His reaping machine could do the work of many men, and it could do it a lot faster. Together with the steel plow and the advent of windmills for irrigation, the Great American Desert was transformed into America's breadbasket.

Shortly after the reaper was invented, the mechanical binder appeared. The binder tied grain into sheaves as fast as it was cut. Using the new device, two men and a team of horses could harvest and bind several acres of wheat a day. Next came the steam-driven thresher, which separated grain from the stalks of wheat. And eventually, Deere introduced the first steel plow to be pulled by horses. One invention followed another, and the impact of the Industrial Revolution on agriculture was apparent everywhere.

Something to Do

Before the reaper, farmers harvested their grain using either a scythe, a sickle, or a scythe with a cradle attachment. Find pictures of these implements and make sketches to illustrate how they differed in appearance.

Extension

How did the steel plow and the reaper help seal the fate of the Plains Indians?

Journal Entry
January 21, 1830

I returned from my visit to the cotton mill in low spirits. Although I shall continue to petition Parliament to take action against heartless owners and the deplorable conditions in their factories, I shan't quickly return to that horrible den of misery and child slavery. Safe and warm in the drawing room of my home, I felt guilty as I sank into my comfortable chair in front of the fire. My mind could not shut out the image of those poor children toiling away, many of them chained to their machines. The hopeless yet pleading look in their eyes pierced my very soul.

I was especially saddened to hear of the death of little Emma. I understand she died from the complications of pneumonia and was bound to her spinning machine almost until the hour she succumbed. Perhaps, however, I should feel joy that such a precious little girl has at last been freed from bondage and has now found peace with her Maker.

Little Emma had been brought into the mill at the age of 5. She was a pauper child bound out to Mr. R. from the local poorhouse. She never received one farthing for the 16 hours a day she labored in that abominable place. If she fell asleep at her machine, she was severely scolded or beaten. Sometimes cold water was thrown in her face to revive her. This she endured six days a week throughout her abbreviated life.

Other children like Emma are sentenced to the same existence. They have no opportunity to go to school or to engage in play. Fresh air is a luxury they never see. Some children are more fortunate, for at least they can return home when their shifts are concluded. These are the children who are unwillingly sentenced to the mill by their parents. But one can't be too harsh on parents for taking such heartrending steps. After all, families must eat.

I have put down my pen, for I can write no more. My heart is broken and tears are streaming down my cheeks. Where do I go now? To the bedrooms of my own children to gaze upon their sleeping countenances and to thank God for my good fortune.

There were two sides to the Industrial Revolution. One was a bright side that saw wonderful advances in machinery, transportation, and communications. The other was a dark side characterized by the evils and abuses of the factory system. This dark side of the revolution was tolerated even in the United States. But it was much worse in Europe.

The factory system robbed skilled workers of their pride and craftsmanship. Forced to work in mills and mines because they could not compete with machines, workers soon became automatons who simply pushed buttons and turned knobs. So simple were the tasks they performed that even the youngest of children could master them. Children, in fact, were preferred over adult workers because their tiny fingers were more adept at operating the machines. And they could be paid much less than adults, or as in the case of children bound out from orphanages, nothing at all. It is small wonder that many of these youngsters grew up anemic and vicious. Robbed of their childhood and deprived of love and education, how else could they have turned out?

Continued on page 19.

The previous paragraphs provide you with a good idea of what it was like to work in the mills and mines of the eighteenth and nineteenth centuries. Picture workers crammed into noisy, dirty, and poorly ventilated factories and coal mines. Picture those in the cotton mills constantly inhaling the tiny cotton fibers that in time caused many of them to contract cancer and other diseases. Picture those in the coal mines breathing the coal dust that either ruined their health or took their life after a few years. Picture the accidents and deaths that resulted from early machines having no safety devices. And picture the struggle for injured workers to survive in an age before workmen's compensation and accident insurance. Considering these wretched conditions under which they toiled and lived, it is not surprising that workers occasionally sabotaged and destroyed the machines responsible for their tragic plight. When such incidents occurred, however, those deemed guilty were hanged.

You may be wondering why governments permitted the evils and abuses of the factory system to continue unchecked. Why were laws not passed limiting the power of owners and guaranteeing certain rights to workers? In time, such laws were enacted, but for many years, governments followed the economic policy of *laissez faire*. *Laissez faire* is a French term meaning "let alone." And that is exactly the position governments took toward business and industry during the Industrial Revolution. The *laissez faire* theory of economics held that business and industry functioned best with little or no interference from ruling authorities. Factory and mine owners, unencumbered by government restrictions or limitations, were left free to impose their will on the hapless workers in their charge.

Although the majority of owners were heartless and uncaring, a few were not. One who tried to help the worker was Robert Owen, a Welsh-born manufacturer and reformer. In 1799, Owen bought several cotton mills in New Lanark, Scotland, and embarked on a bold experiment. He provided housing for workers and their families and raised their wages. He shortened working hours and did not permit children under the age of ten to work. Instead, he built schools for the younger children of his mill workers. Owen believed it was good business to consider his workers' welfare, and his theories proved him right. To everyone's surprise, his mills turned out to be highly profitable.

Owen was one of a breed of socialists called *Utopian Socialists*. The name is derived from the

Continued on page 20.

mythical island of Utopia of which the Englishman Sir Thomas More wrote in 1516. On More's Utopia, an ideal society existed. Everything was perfect: government, laws, justice, and society. Owen and others envisioned communities established on the principles espoused by More in his sixteenth-century book.

Convinced that an ideal community was possbile, Owen came to America in 1825 and bought the Village of Harmony in Indiana from a religious leader named George Rapp. Rapp and his followers, originally from the kingdom of Württemberg in Germany, had founded the community in 1814. Owen renamed it New Harmony and established what he hoped would become an ideal agricultural society.

Internal conflicts doomed New Harmony from the start. The idea of socialism, where property is owned in common by all the people, did not appeal to every inhabitant of the town. Disillusioned, Owen gave up on the project and returned to England after two years. But his experiment served a purpose by representing the efforts of one early reformer to address the evils brought about by the factory system and the Industrial Revolution. Unfortunately, his was a voice in the wilderness for many years to come, as manufacturers and owners continued to reap high profits while completely ignoring the needs of their laborers.

The abuses and conditions Owen and other reformers sought to correct lingered well into the second phase of the Industrial Revolution, which began about the time the Civil War in America ended. Although some owners attempted to improve the lot of their workers, little progress was

made. And the same wretched conditions that existed in the factories and mines of the period were also characteristic of workers' tenements that sprang up in industrial cities everywhere.

Workers' tenements were built almost overnight and of any available material. No building codes regulated where they could or could not be constructed. Tenements were often built next to factories, and workers' familes lived amid the foul air and limited space. Streets were dark, dirty, and dangerous at night. Crime ran rampant, and epidemics of cholera, tuberculosis, typhoid, and other diseases were commonplace.

The influx of workers moving to the cities from rural areas taxed the amount of housing to the limit. It was not unusual to find entire families living in one room. Often the room had no window, and the entire building had no running water or toilet facilities. Raw sewage and waste from factories and mines littered the streets, magnifying the health problems that already existed. Under such deplorable conditions,

Continued on page 21.

it is not surprising that both the death rate and the suicide rate were high. Many young children never lived to see their second birthday.

In desperation, men turned to alcohol, creating an additional social problem. Women, for their part, were equally affected by the wretched conditions under which they lived. Sometimes, to give their shattered nerves a brief respite, mothers gave their babies opium to make them stop crying. In many instances, impoverished parents turned their young children out into the streets to fend for themselves. These pitiful urchins then went from house to house begging for food. Some older ones managed to support themselves by selling newspapers or by becoming bootblacks.

Again, the social problems bred by the Industrial Revolution were not limited to England and other European countries. Many of the same conditions were prevalent in the United States. It's reported that Charles Dickens, the well-known English author whose novels told of the plight of poor children in England, noted on a visit to New York in the 1840s that that city contained as many homeless, starving children as did London. The truth was that every nation touched by the factory system was guilty of permitting deplorable conditions.

Discuss . . .

- how young children—other than health-wise—were adversely affected by employment at a very early age.
- the correlation between poverty and social problems such as alcoholism and crime.
- whether government should exert more or less control over business and industry, and why.
- whether an ideal society, as espoused by Robert Owen and others, is possible. Why or why not?

Extension

There were several reasons why people during the time of the Industrial Revolution were reluctant to come to the aid of the poor—even the pitiful, destitute children who roamed the streets of large cities. One was the Calvinist belief—widely held at the time—that some people were predestined to poverty and were therefore best left alone. Another was the assertion that the poor had none but themselves to blame for their plight.

How do you feel about such beliefs? Do you think people at that time were exceedingly cruel and heartless, more so than people today? Write a one-page paper expressing your thoughts on the subject.

Nottingham, England
August 22, 1833

I am utterly dumfounded by Parliament's latest tomfoolery. Its recent Reform Bill will no doubt force me to close my doors. Can you imagine a bill prohibiting the hiring of children under the age of nine to work in factories? The majority of my workers are under that age! What am I to do? I see nothing but financial ruin ahead.

Factory and mine owners in England were alarmed when reformers in the early 1800s began to call for legislation to address the abuses caused by the Industrial Revolution. They believed that reform laws would put them out of business. But, as matters turned out, legislation that was eventually enacted had little effect on either their output or their profits.

Factory laws to regulate child labor in English factories were passed as early as 1802. But the first law actually enforced cleared Parliament in 1833. The Factory Act of that year forbade the employment of children under the age of 9 in cotton mills. It also set a 9-hour workday for children ages 9 to 13 and a 12-hour workday for those 13 to 18 years of age. Another law passed in 1842 set the same provisions for mines. About the same time, demands were being made for laws requiring compulsory schooltime for children. This then reduced the number of hours children could work.

Similar laws went into effect in the United States. Connecticut in 1813 passed a law requiring that working children receive some education. In 1836, Massachusetts decreed that all children under 15 go to school three months a year. But in spite of state efforts, young children in America continued well into the 1900s to work long hours in factories and at other unhealthy and dangerous jobs. For many years, the law was tilted in favor of manufacturers. Two child labor laws passed by Congress in 1916 and 1918 were declared unconstitutional by the Supreme Court. Its reason for striking down the legislation? The justices declared that both laws not only infringed on states' rights but "interfered with children's right to contract for work." It was not until 1938 when, as part of the Fair Labor Standards Act, a minimum age for children to work was set at 14, with 16 being the minimum age for employment during school hours. The same law established a minimum wage for all workers at 25 cents an hour, gradually moving to 40 cents an hour, and limited the work week to 44 hours.

Workers also benefited from the efforts of labor unions. At first, unions everywhere were banned because of strikes and sabotage inititiated by laborers. But in time, governments began to recognize unions as legal. Great Britain lifted the ban on such organizations in 1824. In 1859, the British government permitted picketing, and 12 years later, strikes.

The union movement grew more slowly in other countries. In the United States, unionism became associated with socialism and anarchism, and every effort was made to stamp it out. Not until 1869 was the first major labor union—the Knights of Labor—recognized. It was followed in 1886 by the American Federation of Labor. The first major strike in the United States was the Great Railroad Strike of 1877.

Discuss . . .

- at what age children are both physically and emotionally ready for full-time employment. Do you feel this age should vary from child to child?

- whether it is fair to deny full-time employment to children under 16.

- what benefits a child might derive from a part-time job.

- when strikes may be detrimental to a nation's welfare.

Promontory, Utah
May 10, 1869

My Dear Clara,

We've done it! The transcontinental railroad is a reality. This afternoon, the golden spike linking the two lines was driven in, ending six years of grueling work against what seemed at times insurmountable odds. Six years of heat, cold, landslides, snowstorms, death, stampeding buffalo, and attacking Indians are finally behind us.

Today's linking of the two lines will be etched in my mind forever. As the engines of the Union Pacific and Central Pacific touched cowcatchers, the final railroad tie of California laurel was driven into place with the golden spike. The whole country could listen as the telegraph lines delivered each blow of the silver sledgehammer used to drive it in. It's been a momentous event for all here. Do you think folks back home felt that way as well?

I must go and attend to some final matters. Kiss the children for me, and give my greetings to your mother. I hope to be home in two or three weeks.

Love,
James

Chicago, Illinois
May 24, 1869

My dearest James,

I realize that you may well be on your way home by the time this letter is delivered, but I wanted to write and tell you how the news of the railroad's completion was received.

Here in Chicago, there was a huge parade that stretched for seven miles. In Washington, a magnetic ball dropped from a pole on top of the Capitol when the news was received. And everywhere there was cheering, bells clanging, and fire sirens shrieking. Everyone is aware of the importance of this event. At long last, the nation is tied together. Uncle Jacob's eyes fill with dollar signs as he thinks of the future and the increased demand for furniture that the railroad must surely bring. After all, those folks who have moved onto the Great Plains are probably tired of sitting on box crates and sleeping on the floor!

I pray for your safe return and hope to see you soon.

All my love,
Clara

Continued on page 24.

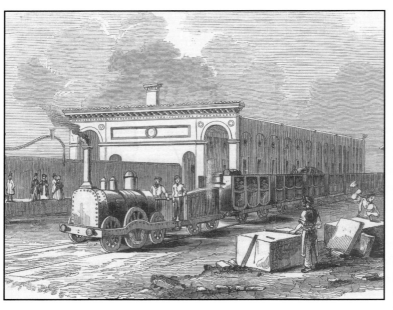

The transcontinental railroad was indeed an event of national importance. It was soon followed by four other railroads that spanned the country, helping to launch a second Industrial Revolution. The railroad made it possible to ship goods to anywhere in America, which led to an increased demand for products of all kinds. This in turn resulted in a tremendous expansion of business and industry, characterized by such new developments as mass production and the assembly line.

The period after the Civil War to the turn of the twentieth century is known in history by various names. Some historians call it the Economic Revolution; others prefer to call it the Age of Steel and Steam. Still others have called it the Gilded Age, the Age of Extremes (between rich and poor), or the Second Industrial Revolution. By whatever name it is known, the period saw some industries expand to become giant monoplies that put their smaller competition out of business. Standard Oil and the Carnegie Steel Company were two of these. The men who used any and all means to build such financial empires—and trampled on their underpaid workers in the process—will be covered in detail in a separate unit.

The Second Industrial Revolution saw many changes take place in America and elsewhere. One was a growth of cities, just as had occurred in the First Industrial Revolution. But this time, the growth was accompanied by innovations that people who had lived 100 years earlier could never have envisioned. Street lights, elevated trains, and trolleys became commonplace in larger cities. So did bicycles and, in time, automobiles. Department stores sprang up and mail-order catalogues did a booming business. It was a wonderful, glorious time for most people.

For others, the Second Industrial Revolution brought many of the same problems as the first. Crowded tenements, poverty, and crime were the bane of every large city, as were sweatshops and "home industries" where entire families worked from dawn until well into the night to earn pennies a day. The problems and abuses associated with this second phase of the Industrial Revolution are covered on future pages.

Discuss . . .

- why mass production is advantageous to consumers.
- why the second phase of the Industrial Revolution is sometimes called "The Gilded Age." (Mark Twain applied that label to the period.)
- why the second Industrial Revolution would lead to another race for colonies on the part of some industrialized nations.

For Debate

Resolved: That superstores (those combining, for example, a supermarket, pharmacy, and possibly a department store) constitute monopolies and should therefore be disallowed.

Chicago, Illinois
July 12, 1888
Dear Diary,

The end of another day, and Josef is in bed. Every night he comes home from the stockyards, wolfs down his supper, and collapses in bed. It is the same scene six nights a week. He spends Sundays sleeping. Although I hunger for conversation, I can't say that I blame the poor man with 12-hour days of sickening odors and unbearable heat. With the only break a rushed lunch, I fear for his health and constantly worry for his safety. I feel often that we should never have left the farm, never have emigrated here.

Yes, accidents happen at the yards and in the plant. I have learned much more than what Josef tells me. I know, for example, that men who work in the tank rooms with open vats at floor level sometimes fall into the bubbling cauldrons. By the time they are fished out, what was once their bones have gone out in containers labeled "Durham's Pure Leaf Lard"! I also know that men have had fingers and hands eaten away by acid or chopped off by the machines they operate. I also know that many suffer from diseases that have come from the vile conditions under which they work.

But do the robber barons care? Does it bother them to give parties at which a guest might find a pearl in an oyster or gold bracelet wrapped around a napkin while their workers are starving? Does it bother Mr. Armour and the others that both of my lovely children died before they were ten—deaths that could have been prevented with proper food and medicine?

Of course not! These heartless men care nothing for the plight of workers and their families. They think of one thing only: MONEY. And those who make the laws are in perfect agreement with them.

A relatively small number of industrialists built huge empires and accumulated vast wealth in the years following the Civil War. The first to do so were railroad tycoons like Cornelius Vanderbilt, Leland Stanford, and James J. Hill. Others who amassed fortunes could thank the railroads, for it was the expansion of the railways that spurred the growth of other industries. Chief among these were steel, oil, processed foods, metals, and communications. An abundance of capital and resources, together with the government's policy of nonintervention, enabled entrepreneurs such as Andrew Carnegie and John D. Rockefeller to become millionaires many times over.

The aforementioned "captains of industry," along with others like Jay Gould and the banker J. P. Morgan, acquired their financial empires through ability and hard work. Their ingenuity and drive helped transform America from an agrarian society into an industrial power. And nearly all were philanthropists who gave millions to charity.

But there was another side to these giants of manufacturing. Most used any and all methods to put their competition out of business and create colossal empires. John D. Rockefeller managed to combine all of his numerous companies and plants into a large industrial monopoly called a *trust*. Other industrialists followed suit, making it possible for them to control production and prices. Because they cared little for the welfare of their workers and seemed interested only in making money, people often referred to them as "robber barons."

Discuss . . .

• whether those industrialists known as "robber barons" subscribed to the principle of "the end justifies the means." Do you agree with such a principle?

• whether—had you been one of the robber barons—you would have felt any obligation to improve the lot of your workers. Explain.

For Further Research

A number of economic terms are associated with the second phase of the Industrial Revolution. Research the following terms: monopoly; division of labor; assembly line; free enterprise; entrepreneur.

Boston, Massachusetts
August 3, 1890

Dear Nina,

Like many who came to America with great hopes, I have found that "all that glitters is not gold." Unlike Vasilly, who I know has written several letters to friends in the village boasting of his "wonderful job" and "luxurious living quarters," I will tell you the truth. Do not come. Stay in Russia. Life in the village is no worse than conditions here. And in the village, at least you are among your own kind.

I live in a dilapidated tenement with no heat and a roof that leaks. I lodge with a family of eight who have an apartment of five rooms. They live in two of the rooms and rent the other three. I live in a small room surrounded on both sides by two surly men who speak to no one and who frighten me to death. Thirty-five people live in this building and share one toilet in the basement. You can imagine the odor and filth surrounding that area.

My job is as unappealing as my room in the tenement. Seven days a week I work from dawn to dusk washing cars in the railroad yards—all for fourteen cents an hour! What kind of job is that for a young woman? I have wanted to go to night school to study English, hoping that a better knowledge of the language would help me find another job. But I am afraid to go out alone at night; the streets are so dangerous.

Nina, heed my advice. Pay no attention to Vasilly's glowing letters. Do not come to America. Stay in Russia.

Your dearest friend,
Olga

A large majority of the workers who toiled in America's factories, mines, and "sweatshops" during the Second Industrial Revolution were immigrants from southern and eastern Europe. Owners preferred to hire them because they would work for lower wages, and the immigrants themselves were eager to take any job they could find. And because their pay was so low, these newcomers to America were forced to live under the worst possible conditions.

The letter above describes a typical tenement in a large city. As you can see, living conditions had improved little since the days of the first Industrial Revolution. Houses and tenements were filled to capacity, with families renting extra rooms to help pay the bills. It is not surprising that disease and crime flourished under such conditions.

Some men came to America alone, hoping to make their "fortunes" and return to their families in the old country. They were called "birds of passage." As such, they paid as little for lodging as possible. Some shared one room in an apartment with as many as 12 other men. They spread mattresses on the floor in rows, there being nothing

Continued on page 27.

else in the room except a stove. Sometimes two men shared the same mattress. The man who worked during the day used the mattress at night, while the night worker claimed it during the day.

Sweatshops were makeshift factories set up in sheds or tenement houses when factories could not house all of the workers. Some sweatshops were of the home variety, where entire families labored from dawn to well into the night trying to earn enough money for life's barest necessities.

Most sweatshops were concentrated in the garment industry. "Sweaters" bought or rented sewing machines and set up shop in tenements. Often, an entire family, its boarders, and nearby neighbors toiled away in several dark rooms for as long as 16 hours a day. Their job was to sew together pre-cut pieces of garments: fronts, backs,

sleeves, cuffs, and so on. Even the youngest of children helped by performing such simple tasks as threading needles and snipping off loose threads. A hard-working child could add from 50¢ to $1.50 a week to a family's income.

Other familes worked equally long hours in their pathetic apartments making such things as cigars and artificial flowers. What they earned for their efforts barely put food on the table. Making artificial flowers, a family had to make 144 flowers to earn 10¢! As in the garment sweatshops, children worked alongside their parents. There was little time for play or school.

In time, laws were passed making sweatshops illegal. But for many years, they were as much a part of the manufacturing scene as factories.

Discuss . . .

- whether you would have canceled plans to come to America had you received a letter similar to the fictitious one Nina received from Olga. Why or why not?

- why slums develop in large cities.

- why immigrant workers from a particular country segregated themselves from other nationalities in the slums.

- whether sweatshops have truly disappeared in the United States.

- what countries that still allow sweatshops have been in the news recently.

For Further Study

Mill owners in Lowell, Massachusetts, in the early 1800s hired young farm girls to work in their factories and boarded them in dormitories. Explain how the treatment of these girls differed from the working conditions associated with the factory system of the late 1800s, described in this unit.

New Orleans, Louisiana
September 12, 1911

Dear Sara,

I have decided to stay over in New Orleans for a day before heading home. The rest will do me good, and it will afford me the opportunity to take in the sights.

Yesterday, I completed my work in the seafood canneries along the Gulf Coast. The pictures I took will reveal to what extent child labor flourishes here. Surely, my photographs will give the National Child Labor Committee much-needed ammunition in its fight for stronger child labor law enforcement. I must say that I was shocked by what I photographed.

In Biloxi, Mississippi, I came upon a lad of five working in a cannery as a shrimp picker. He told me he goes to work at three o'clock every morning and works all day peeling the shells off iced shrimp. He is a sad little boy who has worked at the cannery for more than a year.

In Dunbar, Louisiana, I photographed four-year-old Lisa, who was shucking oysters in a cannery. Her mother, who also works in the cannery, told me little Lisa shucks two pots of oysters a day. Her tiny fingers bear the scars of numerous cuts received from the rough, sharp oyster shells.

Although the conditions I witnessed in the canneries are shocking, they are no more so than conditions elsewhere throughout the country. North, South, East, or West—it makes little difference. As you know from your trips with me, children everywhere are being exploited by uncaring owners and bosses. I have seen it in the cotton mills of New England and the textile mills in the South. I have seen it in the glass factories of Virginia and the coal mines of Pennsylvania. I have witnessed it from Maine to Texas. I dare say, not a state in this Union can boast that it does not tolerate the exploitation of children.

I must close for now and attend to my equipment. I hope to be home within the week.

Love,
Lewis

Continued on page 29.

Photographer Lewis Hine did not write the above letter to his wife in 1911, but he might have written a similar one. For ten years, Hine traveled throughout the country, photographing instances of child labor in America. During that time, he must have written numerous letters to Mrs. Hine describing the conditions he had seen.

Lewis Hine was a schoolteacher who quit his job to become an investigative photographer for the National Child Labor Committee. Concealing his small box camera under his coat, he often posed as a fire inspector or insurance salesman to gain entrance to mills, mines, and other factories where children were employed. His caution and disguises were necessary in an age when inquisitive reformers were not welcome in the nation's workplaces. More than a few were roughed up and told to mind their own business.

Hine and other reformers were hard at work in the early twentieth century trying to put an end to child labor in America. Although most states had enacted some child labor laws, these laws were seldom enforced. Manufacturers used their influence with state legislatures to circumvent all legislation regulating the hiring of children.

Children in the late nineteenth and early twentieth centuries were not chained to machines as were their counterparts 100 years earlier, but they were mistreated and abused in other ways. Young girls and boys who worked as spinners and doffers in cotton mills had water thrown into their faces to keep them awake during their long shifts. And the boys who worked in the breakers of the coal mines were often rapped with broom handles when they showed signs of nodding off on the job.

Child labor was slow to disappear in America. Not until the 1930s was effective national legislation enacted to combat its evils. Compulsory education laws requiring children to attend school until the age of 16 also helped put an end to the hiring of youngsters on a full-time basis.

Unfortunately, child labor remains a problem in other areas of the world. The International Labor Organization of the United Nations reported in 1997 that millions of young children were working as virtual slaves. At least 15% of Asian children between 10 and 14 years of age are working full-time. In India, Pakistan, and Nepal, the numbers may be as high as one million. Many of these are children whose poor parents have literally sold them to employers. With little government intervention, these children have no hope for the future.

Discuss . . .

- whether, as an impoverished parent, you could bring yourself to sell a child into permanent servitude.
- why an advanced and democratic nation such as the United States would allow child labor to have continue well into the 1930s.
- whether the employment of teens on either a part-time or full-time basis causes unemployment among certain adult groups.

For Debate

Resolved: That the United Nations impose economic sanctions on any member nation that tolerates child labor.

Washington, D.C.
June 26, 1938

Yesterday marked a milestone in the history of American labor. The passage of the Fair Labor Standards Act corrects, at long last, abuses in industry that have existed since Samuel Slater built his cotton mill in Rhode Island almost 150 years ago.

This act establishes a minimum wage of 25¢ an hour and sets the work week at 44 hours in interstate industries. It also provides for "time and a half" rates for overtime work. More importantly, it abolishes child labor in industries engaged in interstate commerce.

June 25, 1938, will be remembered as a glorious day in labor's long struggle to secure a fair deal for the American worker.

The emergence of labor unions was mentioned briefly on an earlier page, as was their victory in seeing the Fair Labor Standards Act passed. But a more detailed look is in order if one is to understand the role these organizations played in the progress made by workers everywhere.

The so-called Gilded Age in America's history—those years from the Civil War until the turn of the twentieth century—were violent ones in the labor movement. Strikes and riots were commonplace as management fought every effort on the part of unions to improve working conditions. Many lives were lost as violence troubled the railroad, steel, coal, and Pullman car industries. And in those early years of turmoil, the government usually sided with management.

Conditions began to improve during the first administration of President Franklin D. Roosevelt. Through the efforts of the American Federation of Labor and the Congress of Industrial Organization, which eventually merged into the AFL-CIO in 1955, Congress passed the National Labor Relations Act in 1935. Also called the Wagner Act after its sponsor, this law was the most important piece of legislation ever passed to benefit the American worker.

Among other things, the Wagner Act granted unions the right of collective bargaining. This meant that representatives of unions could sit down and discuss with management such issues as wages, hours, and working conditions. Through collective bargaining, workers not only improved their work environment and pay but also gained such fringe benefits as paid vacations, health insurance, and retirement pensions.

Today, unions continue to represent workers in their relationship with management. Nearly all countries have unions, although they are not as strong in those areas of Africa, Asia, and South America where economics have a more agricultural rather than industrial base.

Discuss . . .

- how unions benefit workers in ways other than just helping them obtain better wages and improved working conditions.
- similarities between labor unions and the craft guilds of the Middle Ages.
- whether unions sometimes put the welfare of the worker ahead of that of the nation as a whole.

For Further Study

Through the years, workers and management have used various "weapons" against each other in their labor disputes. These include the *strike*, the *boycott*, the *lockout*, and the *blacklist*. Look up each term, write its meaning, and tell which side it served as a tactic. Also tell if such action is permitted today.

Tokyo, Japan
December 24, 1997

NEWS BULLETIN

Today, near the city of Kofu, an unmanned, magnetically levitated train (Maglev for short) set a new world speed record of 341 miles per hour. Although the train is not expected to be used commercially for a number of years, its perfor- mance gives passengers an idea of what rail traffic will be like in the future. The new train goes at twice the re- corded speed of present-day "bullet trains." Bullet trains, in turn, currently travel at speeds similar to commer- cial aircraft. This is another major breakthrough in a technology that started with the *DeWitt Clinton,* a 3-mile- per-hour steam locomotive.

In this short book, you have learned some important facts about the first and second Indus- trial Revolutions. Some historians maintain that there have also been a third and a fourth revolu- tion. They insist that the third revolution came about with the advent of the gasoline engine, and that the fourth was a result of the introduction of nuclear power.

In truth, it can be argued that the Industrial Revolution is an ongoing occurrence. Every new invention or way of doing something revolutionizes some aspect of people's lives. It may be an im- proved means of transportation or some innovation in technology. It may be an advancement in com- munications or agriculture. Or it may be a signifi- cant breakthrough in health and medicine. Our lives are continually affected by new developments in every field.

The first two Industrial Revolutions were similar in some ways yet different in others. To compare/ contrast the two, fill in the Venn diagram below. Write several facts or characteristics unique to each revolution in the appropriate place. List features common to both where the sections overlap.

First Industrial Revolution

Both

Second Industrial Revolution

A Chain Reaction (page 12) To turn iron into steel, tremendous heat is used to burn out excess carbon and other impurities. Then, as with the Bessemer process, a variety of pig iron called spiegeleisen is added to strengthen the metal.

The Steam Locomotive (page 15) Events on the time line should be in the following order: Watt's steam engine (1769); Trevithick's locomotive (1804); Stephenson's *The Rocket* (1829); Peter Cooper's *Tom Thumb* (1830); mail first carried by railroad (1831); first sleeping car (1859); transcontinental railroad in U.S. (1869).

Improvements in Communication (page 16) *volt*: a standard measure of electrical force used in causing a flow of current along wires; *ampere*: unit for measuring the strength of an electric current; *watt*: a measure of electrical power; *ohm*: a measure of electrical resistance.

The Robber Barons (page 25) *monopoly*: single control over all the supply of a product; *division of labor*: condition in which each worker is skilled in a single operation; *assembly line*: row of workers and machines along which work is passed until the final product is completed; *free enterprise*: economic system based upon the private ownership of property operating in competitive marketplace, based on demands of consumer with limited government interference; *entrepreneur*: person who owns and runs a business.

Slums and Sweatshops (page 27) The girls who worked in the cotton mills of Lowell lived in chaperoned boarding houses and were well-paid for their work. This was in contrast to later factories where workers were poorly paid and lived in crowded tenements.

The Role of Labor (page 30) *strike*: an organized work stoppage; *boycott*: to refuse to do business with; *lockout*: when a plant is closed by its owner to prevent employees from working during a labor dispute; *blacklist*: a list of undesirable workers drawn up by employers. Strikes and boycotts were weapons of labor, while blacklists and lockouts were used by management. Blacklists are disallowed today.

Select Bibliography

Blumenthal, Shirley. *Coming to America: Immigrants from Eastern Europe.* New York: Delacorte Press, 1981.

Freedman, Russell. *Kids at Work: Lewis Hine and the Crusade Against Child Labor.* New York: Clarion Books, 1994.

Groner, Alex, and the editors of American Heritage and Business Week. *The American Heritage History of Business and Industry.* New York: American Heritage Publishing Co., Inc., 1972.

Hakim, Joy. *A History of U.S.: The New Nation.* New York: Oxford University Press, 1995.

Toynbee, Arnold. *The Industrial Revolution.* Gloucester, Massachusetts: Peter Smith, 1990.

Toynton, Evelyn. *Growing Up in America: 1830–1860.* Brookfield, Connecticut: The Millbrook Press, 1995.

Vialls, Christine. *The Industrial Revolution Begins.* Minneapolis: Lerner Publications Company, 1982.